SONGS IN THE NIGHT

The New Park Street Pulpit.

SONGS IN THE NIGHT

———

A Sermon

Intended for Reading on Lord's-day, February 27th, 1898.

Originally delivered by

Charles H. Spurgeon

at the New Park Street Chapel, Southwark.

———

Where is God my Maker, who gives songs in the night?—Job 35:10.

Updated to modern language by Charles J. Doe

[CURIOSMITH]

Minneapolis

Published by Curiosmith.
Minneapolis, Minnesota.
Internet: curiosmith.com.

Previously published by SHELDON, BLAKEMAN & COMPANY in 1857.

The text of this edition is from sermon number 2558, Volume 44 of
The Metropolitan Tabernacle Pulpit, 1898. Passages from *The World's
Great Sermons* compiled by Grenville Kleiser, and *Pulpit Eloquence of
the Nineteenth Century* by Henry C. Fish, that were left out of *The
Metropolitan Tabernacle Pulpit* text, are compiled into this edition.

The text was updated to modern equivalents of Elizabethan and Victorian
words and phrases. Occasional occurrences of lengthy sentences and close
punctuation were left unchanged.

The "Guide to the Contents" was added to this edition by the publisher.

ISBN 9781941281086

GUIDE TO THE CONTENTS

———o◦¡◦¡◦o———

SONGS IN THE NIGHT

CHARLES H. SPURGEON

*But none says, Where is God my Maker, who gives
songs in the night?*—JOB 35:10.

Elihu was a wise man, exceedingly wise,
though not as wise as the all-wise Jehovah,
who sees light in the clouds and finds order
in confusion. For this reason Elihu, being much
puzzled at seeing Job afflicted, searched to find the
cause of it and he very wisely hit upon one of the
most likely reasons, although it did not happen to
be the right one in Job's case. He said within himself, "Surely, if men are sorely tried and troubled,
it is because while they think about their troubles
and distress themselves about their fears, they do
not say, 'Where is God my Maker, who gives songs
in the night?'" Elihu's reason is right in the major-
ity of cases. The great cause of a Christian's distress,
the reason of the depths of sorrow into which many

believers are plunged is simply this—that while they are looking about, on the right hand and on the left, to see how they may escape their troubles, they forget to look to the hills, from where all real help comes; they do not say, "Where is God my Maker, who gives songs in the night?"

We shall, however, leave that inquiry and dwell upon those sweet words, "God my Maker, who gives songs in the night." The world has its night. It seems necessary that it should have one. The sun shines by day and people go forth to their labors; but they grow weary and nightfall comes on, like a sweet present from heaven. The darkness draws the curtains, and shuts out the light, which might prevent our eyes from slumber; while the sweet, calm stillness of the night permits us to rest upon the bed of ease, and there forget our cares awhile, until the morning sun appears, and an angel puts their hand upon the curtain, opens it once again, touches our eyelids, and invites us to rise and proceed to the labors of the day. Night is one of the greatest blessings people enjoy; we have many reasons to thank God for it. Yet night is to many a gloomy season. There is "the pestilence that stalks in the darkness"; there is "the terror of night";[1] there is the dread of robbers and of cruel disease, with all those fears that the timid know, when they have no light by which they can discern different objects. It is then

1 See Psalm 91:5, 6 (NIV).

they fancy that spiritual creatures walk the earth; though, if they knew rightly, they would find it to be true that—

"Millions of spiritual creatures walk the earth
Unseen, both when we wake, and when we sleep,"[1]

and that at all times they are around *us*, not more by night than by day. Night is the season of terror and alarm to most people; yet even night has its songs. Have you ever stood by the seaside at night and heard the pebbles sing, and the waves chant *God's* praises? Or have you ever risen from your bed and thrown up the window of your room, and listened there? Listened to what? Silence—except now and then a murmuring sound, which seems sweet music then. And haven't you fancied that you have heard the harp of God playing in heaven? Didn't you conceive that those *stars*—that *those* eyes of God looking down on you—were also mouths of *song* and that every star was singing *God's* glory, singing as it shone, to its mighty Maker, and his rightful, well-deserved praise? Night has its songs. We do not need much poetry in our spirit to catch the song of night and hear the spheres as they chant praises which are loud to the heart, though they be silent to the ear—the praises of the mighty God who bears up the unpillared arch of heaven, and

1 A quote from *Paradise Lost* by John Milton.

moves the *stars* in their courses.

People too, like the great world in which they live, must have their night. For it is true that a person is like the world around them; they are themselves a little world; they resemble the world in almost everything; and if the world has its night, so has its people. And many a night do we have—nights of sorrow, nights of persecution, nights of doubt, nights of bewilderment, nights of affliction, nights of anxiety, nights of ignorance, nights of all kinds which press upon our spirits and terrify our souls. But blessed be God, the Christian can say, "My God gives me songs in the night."

It is not necessary, I take it, to prove to you that Christians have nights; for if you are a Christian, you will find that *you* have them, and you will not want any proof, for nights will come quite often enough. I will, therefore, proceed at once to the subject; and I will speak this evening about songs in the night, first, *their source*—God gives them; secondly, *their matter*—what do we sing about in the night? thirdly, *their excellence*—they are hearty songs, and they are sweet ones; and fourthly, *their uses*—their benefits to ourselves and others.

I. First, songs in the night—who IS THE AUTHOR OF THEM? *"God,"* says the text. Our "Maker," *he* gives songs in the night.

Any person can sing in the day. When the cup is full, a person draws inspiration from it; when wealth rolls in abundance around them, any person can sing to the praise of a GOD who gives a plentiful harvest, or sends home a loaded argosy.[1] It is easy enough for an Aeolian harp[2] to whisper music when the winds blow; the difficulty is for music to come when no wind blows. It is easy to sing when we can read the notes by daylight, but the skillful singer is one who can sing when there is no ray of light by which to read—who sings from their heart, and not from a book that they can see, because they have no means of reading, except from that inward book of their own living spirit, from which notes of gratitude pour out in songs of praise. No person can make a song in the night themselves; they may attempt it, but they will find how difficult it is. When all things please me—I will weave songs, weave them wherever I go, with the flowers that grow upon my path; but put me in a desert, where no flowers are, and with what shall I weave a chorus of praise to God? How shall I make a crown for him? Let this voice be free, and this body be full of health, and I can sing God's praise; but stop this tongue, lay me upon the bed of weakness, and it is not so easy to sing from the bed, and chant high praises in the fires. Give me the bliss of spiritual liberty, and let me ascend up to my God, get near

---

1 Argosy—a large ship, especially a merchant vessel of the largest size.
2 Aeolian harp—a stringed instrument played by the wind.

the throne, and I will sing, yes, sing as sweet as seraphs; but confine me, restrain my spirit, clip my wings, make me exceeding sad, so that I become old like the eagle—then it is hard to sing! It is not in a person's power to sing in trouble. *"Bless* the Lord, O my Soul, and all that is within me bless his holy name," for that is a daylight song. But it was a divine song which Habakkuk sang when, in the night he said, "Though the fig tree does not bud," and so on, "yet I will rejoice in the LORD, I will be joyful in God my Savior."[1] I think on the far edge of the Red Sea, any man could have made a song like that of Moses, "The horse and his rider he has thrown into the sea";[2] the difficulty would have been to compose a song before the Red Sea had been divided, and to sing it before Pharaoh's hosts had been drowned, while yet the darkness of doubt and fear was resting on Israel's multitudes. Songs in the night come only from God; they are not in the power of a person.

But what does the text mean when it asserts that God gives songs in the night? We think we find two answers to the question. The first *is,* that usually in the night of a Christian's experience, *God is their only song.* If it is daylight in my heart, I can sing songs touching my graces, songs touching my sweet experiences, songs touching my duties,

1 See Habakkuk 3:17–18 (NIV).
2 See Exodus 15:21.

songs touching my labors; but let the night come, my graces appear to have withered; my evidences, though they are there, are hidden; I can not

> "Read my title clear
> To mansions in the skies";[1]

and now I have nothing left to sing of but my God. It is strange, that when God gives his children mercies, they generally set their hearts more on the mercies than on the Giver of them; but when the night comes, and he sweeps all the mercies away, then at once they each say, "Now, my God, I have nothing to sing of but you; I must come to you and to you only. I had cisterns[2] once; they were full of water and I drank from them then; but now the created streams are dry; sweet Lord, I drink from no stream but your own *Self,* I drink from no fountain but from you." *Yes,* child of God, you know what I say; or, if you do not yet understand it, you will do so in the future! It is in the night we sing of God and of God alone. Every string is tuned and every power has its tribute of song while we praise God and nothing else. We can sacrifice to ourselves in daylight; we only sacrifice to God by

1 A quote from *When I Can Read My Title Clear* by Isaac Watts.

2 Cistern—an artificial or natural reservoir; a hollow place containing water or other liquids.

night. We can sing high praises to ourselves when all is joyful, but we cannot sing praise to any but our God when circumstances are troublesome and providences appear adverse. God alone can furnish us with songs in the night.

And yet again, not only does God give the song in the night, because he is the only subject upon which we can sing then, but because *he is the only One who inspires songs in the night.* Bring me a poor, melancholy, *distressed* child of God. From the pulpit, I seek to tell them precious promises, and whisper to them sweet words of comfort; they do not listen to me; they are like the deaf serpent, they do not heed the voice of the charmer, however wisely they are charmed. Send them around to all the comforting clergymen and all the holy Barnabases who ever preached, and they will do very little with them; they will not be able to squeeze a song out of them, do what they may. They are drinking gall and wormwood;[1] they say, "O Lord, I have eaten ashes like bread, and mingled my drink with weeping";[2] and comfort them as you may, it will be only a faint note or two of mournful resignation that you will get from them; you will not evoke psalms of praise, no hallelujahs, no joyful sonnets. But let God come to his child in the

---

1 Gall and wormwood—extremely disagreeable and bitter tasting substances.
2 Psalm 102:9.

night, let him whisper in their ear as they lie on their bed, and now you can see their eyes light up brightly in the night! Don't you hear them say,—

> "'Tis Paradise, if thou are here;
> If thou depart, 'tis hell?"[1]

I could not have cheered them—it is God that has done it; for God "gives songs in the night." It is marvelous, brothers and sisters, how one sweet word of God will make many songs for Christians. One Word of God is like a piece of gold, and the Christian is the goldsmith, and they can hammer that promise out for whole weeks. I can say myself, I have lived on one promise for weeks, and wanted no other. I had just simply to hammer the promise out into gold-leaf, and plate my whole existence with joy from it. The Christian gets their songs from God; God gives them inspiration and teaches them how to sing: "God my Maker, who gives songs in the night."

So then, poor Christian, you do not need to pump up your poor heart to make it glad. Go to your Maker, and ask him to give you a song in the night. You are a poor dry well; you have heard it said that when a pump is dry, you must pour water down it first of all, and then you will get some up. So Christian, when you are dry, go to your God, ask

1 A quote from *God All, and in All* by Isaac Watts.

him to pour some joy down you, and then you will get more joy up from your own heart. Do not go to this comforter or that, for you will find them "Job's comforters" after all; but go first and foremost to your Maker, for he is the great Composer of songs and Teacher of music. It is he who can teach you how to sing, "God, my Maker, who gives me songs in the night."

II. So far we have dwelt upon the first point; now we turn to the second. WHAT IS GENERALLY THE MATTER CONTAINED IN A SONG IN THE NIGHT? What do we sing about?

Why, I think, when we sing by night, there are three things we sing about. Either we sing about the day that is over, or about the night itself, or else about the day that is to come. Those are all sweet themes when God our Maker gives us songs in the night. In the middle of the night, the most usual method for Christians is to sing about *the day that is over.* "Well," they say, "it is night now, but I can remember when it was daylight. Neither moon nor stars appear at present, but I remember when I saw the sun. I have no evidence just now, but there was a time when I could say, 'I know that my Redeemer lives.' I have my doubts and fears at this present moment, but it is not long since I could say with full assurance, 'I know that he shed his blood for me. I know that my Redeemer lives, and when he shall stand a second time upon the earth, though the worms devour this body, yet in my flesh I shall see God.' It may be darkness now, but I know the promises *were* sweet; I know I had blessed seasons in his house. I am quite sure of this—I used to enjoy myself in the ways of the Lord; and though now my path is strewn with thorns, I know it is the King's highway. It was a way of pleasantness once; it will be a way of pleasantness again. 'I will remember the years of the right hand of the Most High.'"[1] Christian, perhaps the best song you can sing, to cheer you in the night, is the song of yesterday. Remember, it was not always night with you; night is a new thing to you. Once you had a glad heart and a buoyant spirit; once your eyes were full of fire; once your foot was light; once you could sing for very joy and ecstasy of heart. Well then, remember that God who made you sing yesterday has not left you in the night. He is not a daylight God who cannot know his children in darkness, but he loves you now as much as ever. Though he has left you for a little while, it is to prove you, to make you trust him more and love and serve him more. Let me tell you some of the sweet things of which a Christian may make a song when it is night with them.

If we are going to sing of the things of yesterday, let us begin with what God did for us in past

---

1 See Psalm 77:10. God's "right hand" refers to his power and authority.

times. My beloved brothers and sisters, you will find it a sweet subject for song at times to begin to sing of electing love and covenant mercies. When you yourself, are low, it is well to sing of the Fountain-head of mercy; of that blessed decree in which you were ordained to eternal life, and of that glorious Man who undertook your redemption; of that solemn covenant signed, sealed, and ratified, in all things ordered well; of that everlasting love which, before the ancient mountains were born, or before the aged hills were children, chose you, loved you firmly, loved you fast, loved you well, loved you eternally. I tell you, believer, if you can go back to the years of eternity—if you can in your mind run back to that period before the everlasting hills were fashioned, or the fountains of the great deep were scooped out, and if you can see your God inscribing your name in his eternal Book—if you can read in his loving heart eternal thoughts of love to you, you will find this a charming means of giving you songs in the night. There are no songs like those which come from electing love; no sonnets like those that are dictated by meditations on discriminating mercy. Some, indeed, cannot sing of election: the Lord open their mouths a little wider! Some are afraid of the very term; but we only despise people who are afraid of what they believe, afraid of what God has taught them in his Bible. No, in our darker hours it is our joy to sing:

"Sons we are through God's election,
    Who in Jesus Christ believe;
By eternal destination,
    Sovereign grace we now receive.
Lord, thy favor,
    Shall both grace and glory give."[1]

Think, Christian, of the eternal covenant, and you will get a song in the night. But if you do not have a voice tuned to so high a key as that, let me suggest some other mercies you may sing of—the mercies you have experienced. What! Can't you sing a little of that blessed hour when Jesus met you; when you were a blind slave making sport of death. He saw you and said, "Come, poor slave, come with Me"? Can't you sing of that rapturous moment when he snapped your fetters,[2] dashed your chains to the earth and said, "I am the Breaker; I am come to break your chains and set you free"? Though you are now ever so gloomy, can you forget that happy morning when, in the house of God, your voice was loud, almost as a seraph's voice, in praise, for you could sing, "I am forgiven! I am forgiven;

A monument of grace,
A sinner saved by blood"?[3]

---

1 A quote from a hymn that appeared in *Gospel Magazine*.
2 Fetter—a chain or shackle for the feet.
3 A quote from *All Mercies Traced to Electing Love* by John Kent.

Go back, sing of that moment and then you will have a song in the night. Or, if you have almost forgotten that, then surely you have some precious milestone along the road of life that is not quite overgrown with moss, on which you can read some happy inscription of God's mercy towards you. What! Did you ever have a sickness like that which you are suffering now, and he did not raise you up from it? Were you ever poor before, and he did not supply your necessities? Were you ever in difficulty before, and he did not deliver you? Come! I plead with you, go to the river of your experience and pull up a few bulrushes and weave them into an ark, in which your infant faith may float safely on the stream. I beg you to not forget what God has done for you. What! Have you buried your diary? I plead with you, turn over the book of your remembrance. Can't you see some sweet hill Mizar? Can't you think of some blessed hour when the Lord met with you at Hermon?[1] Have you ever been on the Delectable Mountains?[2] Have you ever been fetched from the den of lions? Have you ever escaped the jaw of the lion and the paw of the bear? No? Christian, I know you have! Go back then, a little way, to the mercies of the past; and though it is dark now, light up the lamps of yesterday, and they shall glitter through the darkness, and you shall

1 Mizar and Hermon—see Psalm 42:6.
2 A reference to *The Pilgrim's Progress* by John Bunyan.

find that God has given you a song in the night.

"Yes!" says one, "but you know that when we are in the dark, we cannot see the mercies that God has given us. It is all very well for you to tell us this, but we cannot get hold of them." I remember an old experimental[1] Christian speaking about the great pillars of our faith. He was a sailor, and we were on board ship, and there were various huge posts on the shore, to which the vessels were usually fastened, by throwing a cable over them. After I had told him a great many promises, they said, "I know they are good promises, but I cannot get near enough to shore to throw my cable around them; that is the difficulty." Now, it often happens that God's past mercies and loving kindnesses would be secure posts to hold on to, but we do not have enough faith to throw our cable around them, so we go slipping down the stream of unbelief, because we cannot restrain ourselves by our former mercies.

I will, however, give you something over which I think you can throw your cable. If God has never been kind to you, one thing you surely know, and that is—he has been kind to others. Come now, if you are in great difficulties, surely there have been others in greater difficulties. What! are you lower down than poor Jonah was when he went to the bottoms of the mountains? Are you worse off than

---

1 Experimental—known by, or derived from, experience; as, experimental religion.

your Master when he had nowhere to lay his head? What! Do you conceive yourself to be the worst of the worst? Look at Job, scraping himself with a potsherd and sitting on a dunghill. Are you as bad off as he? Yet Job rose up and was richer than before; and out of the depths, Jonah came and preached the Word; and our Savior Jesus has ascended to his throne. Christian! only think of what God has done for others! If you cannot remember that he has done anything for you, remember, I urge you, what his usual rule is and do not judge my God harshly. You remember when Ben-Hadad was overcome and fled, his servants said to him, "Look, we have heard that the kings of Israel are merciful. Let us go to the king of Israel with sackcloth around our waists and ropes around our heads. Perhaps he will spare your life." Wearing sackcloth around their waists and ropes around their heads, they went to the king of Israel and said, "Your servant Ben-Hadad says: 'Please let me live.'" The king answered, "Is he still alive? He is my brother."[1] And truly, poor soul, if you never had a merciful God—others have had a merciful God. The King of Kings is merciful; go and try him. If you are ever so low in your troubles, look to the hills, from where your help comes. Others have had help from there and so may you. Hundreds of God's children might be roused, and show us their hands full of comforts and mercies. They could say, "The Lord

1 1 Kings 20:31–32 (NIV).

gave us these without money and without price; and why shouldn't he give to you also, seeing that you too are the King's son?" In this, Christian, you may get a song in the night out of other people if you cannot get a song from yourself. Never be ashamed of taking a page out of another person's experience book. If you can find no good page in your own, tear one out of someone else's. If you have no cause to be grateful to God in darkness, or cannot find cause in your own experience, go to someone else, and, if you can, praise God in the dark, and like the nightingale, sing his praise sweetly when all the world has gone to rest. We can sing in the night of the mercies of yesterday.

But I think, beloved, a night is never so dark that there is nothing to sing about, even *concerning that night;* for there is one thing I am sure we can sing about, however dark the night, and that is, "Because of the LORD's great love we are not consumed, for his compassions never fail."[1] If we cannot sing very loud, we can sing a little low tune, something like this, "He does not treat us as our sins deserve or repay us according to our iniquities."[2] One says, "I do not know where I shall get my dinner tomorrow; I am a poor miserable person." So you may be, my dear friend, but you are not so poor as you deserve to be. Do not be

1 Lamentations 3:22 (NIV).
2 Psalm 103:10 (NIV).

mightily offended about that; if you are, you are no child of God, for the child of God acknowledges that they have no right to the least of God's mercies, and they come through the channel of grace alone. As long as I am out of hell, I have no right to grumble; and if I were in hell, I should have no right to complain, for I felt, when convinced of sin, that never a creature deserved to go there more than I did. We have no cause to murmur; we can lift up our hands and say, "Night! You are dark, but you might have been darker. I am poor, but if I could not have been poorer, I might have been sick. I am poor and sick, yet I have some friends left; my lot cannot be so bad, but it might have been worse." Therefore, Christian, you will always have one thing to sing about, "Lord, I thank you it is not all darkness!" Besides, however dark the night is, there is always a star or moon. There is scarcely a night that we don't have one or two little lamps burning in the sky. However dark it may be, I think you may find some little comfort, some little joy, some little mercy left, and some little promise to cheer your spirit. The stars are not put out, are they? No, if you cannot see them, they are there, but I think one or two must be shining on you; therefore give God a song in the night. If you have only one star, bless God for that one, and perhaps he will make it two; and if you have only two stars, bless God twice for the two stars, and perhaps he will make them four. Try, then, to find a song in the night.

But, beloved, there is another thing of which we can sing yet more sweetly, and that is we can sing of *the day that is to come.*

I am preaching tonight for the poor weavers of Spitalfields. Perhaps there are not to be found a class of men in London who are suffering a darker night than they are; for while many classes have been befriended and defended, there are few who speak up for them, and (if I am rightly informed) they are generally ground down within an inch of their lives. I suppose that their masters intend that their bread shall be very sweet, on the principle, that the nearer the ground, the sweeter the grass; for I should think that no people have their grass so near the ground as the weavers of Spitalfields. In an inquiry by the House of Commons last week, it was given in evidence that their average wages amount to seven or eight shillings a week; and that they have to furnish themselves with a room, and work at expensive articles, which my friends and ladies are wearing now, and which they buy as cheaply as possible; but perhaps they do not know that they are made with the blood and bones and marrow of the Spitalfields weavers, who, many of them, work for less than a person should to have to subsist upon. Some of them waited upon me the other day; I was exceedingly pleased with one of them.

He said, "Well, sir, it is very hard, but I hope

there are better times coming for us."

"Well, my friend," I said, "I am afraid you cannot hope for much better times, unless the Lord Jesus Christ comes a second time."

"That is just what we hope for," said he. "We do not see there is any chance of deliverance, unless the Lord Jesus Christ comes to establish his kingdom upon the earth; and then he will judge the oppressed, and break the oppressors in pieces with an iron rod, and dash them in pieces like a potter's vessel."

I was glad my friend had got a song in the night, and was singing about the morning that was coming. Often I cheer myself with the thought of the coming of the Lord. We preach now, perhaps, with little success; "the kingdoms of this world" have not yet "become the kingdoms of our God and of his Christ." We send out missionaries, but they are for the most part unsuccessful. We are laboring, but we do not see the fruit of our labor. Well, what then? We shall not always labor in vain, or spend our strength for nothing. A day is coming when every minister of Christ shall speak with unction, when all the servants of God shall preach with power, and when colossal systems of heathenism shall tumble from their pedestals, and mighty, gigantic delusions shall be scattered to the winds. The shout shall be heard, "Alleluia! Alleluia! The Lord God Omnipotent reigns." I look for that day;

it is to the bright horizon of Christ's second coming that I turn my eyes. My anxious expectation is, that the sweet Sun of righteousness will arise with healing beneath his wings, that the oppressed shall be righted, that despotisms shall be cut down, that liberty shall be established, that peace shall be made lasting and that the glorious liberty of the gospel of God shall be extended throughout the known world. Christian! if it is night with you, think of tomorrow; cheer up your heart with the thought of the coming of our Lord. Be patient, for

"Lo, he comes with clouds descending."[1]

Be patient! The farmer waits until he reaps his harvest. Be patient, for you know who has said, "Behold, I am coming soon! My reward is with me, and I will give to everyone according to what he has done."[2]

One more thought upon this point. There is another sweet tomorrow of which we hope to sing in the night. Soon, beloved, you and I shall lie on our dying bed and we shall not lack a song in the night even then; and I do not know where we shall get that song if we do not get it from the tomorrow. Kneeling by the bed of an apparently dying saint recently, I said,

"Well, sister, the Lord has been very precious to

1 Title of a hymn by John Cennick.
2 Revelation 22:12 (NIV).

you; you can rejoice in his covenant mercies and his past loving kindnesses."

She put out her hand and said, "Do not talk about them now! I need the sinner's Savior as much now as ever; it is not a saint's Savior I need; it is still a sinner's Savior that I need, for I am a sinner still."

I found that I could not comfort her with the past, so I reminded her of the golden streets, of the gates of pearl, of the walls of jasper, of the harps of gold, of the songs of bliss; and then her eyes glistened.

She said, "Yes, I shall be there soon; I shall see them in a short time"; and then she seemed so glad!

Believer, you may always cheer yourself with that thought; for if you are ever so low now, remember that

> "A few more rolling suns, at most,
> Will land me on fair Canaan's coast."[1]

Your head may be crowned with thorny troubles now, but it shall wear a starry crown shortly; your hands may be filled with cares, but they shall grasp a harp soon, a harp full of music. Your garments may be soiled with dust now, but they shall be white in the future. Wait a little longer. Beloved! how despicable our troubles and trials will seem when we look back upon them! Looking at them here in

1 A quote from *Christ Our Hiding-place* by John H. Brewer.

the present, they seem immense; but when we get to heaven, we shall then,

> "With transporting joys, recount
> The labors of our feet."[1]

Our trials will seem to us just nothing at all. We shall talk to one another about them in heaven and find all the more to converse about, more according as we have suffered, here below. Let us go on, therefore, and if the night is ever so dark, remember there is not a night that shall not have a morning; and that morning is to come soon. When sinners are lost in darkness, *we* shall lift up our eyes in everlasting light. Surely I need not dwell longer on this thought. There is matter enough for songs in the night in the past, the present and the future.

III. And now I want to tell you, very briefly, WHAT ARE THE EXCELLENCIES OF SONGS IN THE NIGHT ABOVE ALL OTHER SONGS.

In the first place, when you hear a person singing a song in the night—I mean in the night of trouble—you may be quite sure it is a *hearty one.* Many of you sing very heartily now; I wonder whether you would sing as loudly if there were a stake or two in Smithfield[2] for all of you who dared

---

1 A quote from the hymn *The Pilgrimage of the Saints* by Isaac Watts.

2 Smithfield—a very old meat market in London where martyrs were burned at the stake.

to do it. If you sang under pain and penalty, that would show your heart to be in your song. We can all sing very nicely indeed when everybody else sings. It is the easiest thing in the world to open our mouth, and let the words come out, but when the devil puts his hand over our mouth, can we sing then? Can you say, "Though he slay me, yet will I trust in him"?[1] That is hearty singing; that which is real song that springs up in the night. The nightingale sings most sweetly because she sings in the night. We know a poet has said that, if she sang by day, she might be thought to sing no more sweetly than the wren. It is the stillness of the night that makes her song sweet. And so does a Christian's song become sweet and hearty, because it is in the night.

Again, the songs we sing in the night will be *lasting*. Many songs we hear our fellow townspeople singing in the streets will not do to sing in the future. I imagine they will sing a different kind of song soon. They can now sing rollicking drinking songs, but they will not sing them when they come to die; they are not exactly the songs with which to cross Jordan's billows. It will not do to sing one of those light songs when death and you are having the last tug. It will not do to enter heaven singing one of those impure, unholy sonnets. No, but the Christian who can sing in the night will not have

1 See Job 13:15.

to leave off their song; they may keep on singing it forever. They may put their foot in Jordan's stream, and continue their melody; they may wade through it, and keep on singing until they are landed safe in heaven. When they are there, there need not be a pause in their song, but in a nobler, sweeter song they may still continue singing the Savior's power to save. There are a great many of you that think Christian people are a very miserable set, don't you? You say, "Let me sing my song." Yes, but, my dear friends, we like to sing a song that will last; we don't like your songs; they are all froth, like bubbles on the breaker, and they will soon die away and be lost. Give me a song that will last; give me one that will not melt. Don't give me the dreamer's gold! they hoard it up, and say, "I'm rich," and when they awake, their gold is gone. But give me songs in the night, for they are songs I sing forever.

Again, the songs we warble in the night are those that show we have *real faith in God*. Many people have just enough faith to trust God as far as they can see him, and they always sing when they agree with providence; but true faith can sing when its possessors cannot see. It can take hold of God when they cannot discern him.

Songs in the night, too, prove that we have *true courage*. Many sing by day who are silent by night; they are afraid of thieves and robbers, but the Christian who sings in the night is proof they have a courageous character. It is the bold Christian who can sing God's sonnets in the darkness.

A person who can sing songs in the night proves, also that they have *true love to Christ*. It is not love to Christ merely to praise him while everybody else praises him. To walk arm in arm with him when he has the crown on his head, is no great deed. To walk with Christ in rags, is something more. To believe in Christ when he is shrouded in darkness, to stick hard and fast by the Savior when all people speak ill of him and forsake him—that proves true faith. A person who sings a song to Christ in the night, sings the best song in all the world, for they sing from the heart.

IV. I will not dwell further on the excellencies of night songs, but in the last place, SHOW YOU THEIR USE.

Well, beloved, it is very useful to sing in the night of our troubles, first, *because it will cheer ourselves*. When some of you were boys, living in the country, and had some distance to go alone at night, don't you remember how you whistled and sang to keep your courage up? Well, what we do in the natural world, we ought to do in the spiritual. There is nothing like singing to keep up our spirits. When we have been in trouble, we have often thought ourselves to be nearly overwhelmed with difficulty, so we have said, "Let us have a song." We have begun to sing; and we have proved the truth of what Martin Luther says, "The devil cannot bear singing." That is the truth; he doesn't like music. It was so in Saul's day when an evil spirit rested on Saul, but when David played his harp, the evil spirit left him. This is usually the case, and if we can begin to sing, we shall remove our fears. I like to hear servants sometimes humming a tune at their work. I love to hear a farmer in the country singing as he goes along with his horses. Why not? You say he has no time to praise God; but if he can sing a song, surely he can sing a Psalm, it will take no more time. Singing is the best thing to purge ourselves of evil thoughts. Keep your mouth full of songs and you will often keep your heart full of praises; keep on singing as long as you can; you will find it a good method of driving away your fears.

Sing in the night, again, because *God loves to hear his people sing in the night.* At no time does God love his children's singing so well as when they give a serenade of praise under his window, when he has hidden his face from them, and will not appear to them at all. They are all in darkness, but they come under his window and they begin to sing there. God says, "That is true faith that can make them sing praises when I do not appear to them! I know there is faith in them that makes them lift up their hearts, even when I seem to withhold from them all my tender mercies and all my compassions." Sing then, Christian, for singing pleases God. In heaven, we read that the angels are employed in singing, be employed in the same way, for by no better means can you gratify the Almighty One of Israel, who stoops from his high throne to observe us poor, feeble creatures everyday.

Sing again, for another reason; *because it will cheer your companions.* If any of them are in the valley and in the darkness with you, it will be a great help to comfort them. John Bunyan tells us that, as Christian was going through the valley, he found it a dreadful place; horrible demons and goblins were all about him, and poor Christian thought he must perish for certain, but just when his doubts were the strongest, he heard a sweet voice.[1] He listened to it and he heard a man in front of him singing, "Even though I walk through the valley of the shadow of death, I will fear no evil."[2] Now, that man did not know who was near him, but he was unwittingly cheering a pilgrim behind. Christian, when you are in trouble, sing; you do not know who is near you. Sing! perhaps you will get a good companion by it. Sing! perhaps there will be another heart cheered by your song. There is some broken spirit, it may be, that will be bound up by your sonnets. Sing! there is some poor distressed brother or sister, perhaps, shut up in the Castle of Despair, who, like King Richard, will hear your song inside the walls, and sing to you again, and you may be the

1 Refers to *The Pilgrim's Progress* by John Bunyan.
2 Psalm 23:4 (NIV).

means of getting them ransomed and released. Sing Christian, wherever you go; try, if you can, to wash your face every morning in a bath of praise. When you leave your house, never look on anyone till you have first looked on your God; and when you have looked on him, seek to come with a face beaming with joy—carry a smile, for you will cheer up many a poor, wayward pilgrim by it. And when you fast, Christian, when you have an aching heart, do not appear to people to fast; appear cheerful and happy; put oil on your head and wash your face. Be happy for your fellow believer's sake; it will tend to cheer them up and help them through the valley.

One more reason, and I know it will be a good one for you. Try and sing in the night, Christian, for *that is one of the best arguments in all the world in favor of your religion*. Our clergymen, presently, spend a great deal of time in trying to prove the truth of Christianity to those who disbelieve it. I should like to have seen Paul trying that plan! Elymas the sorcerer opposed him; how did Paul treat him? He said, "You are a child of the devil and an enemy of everything that is right! You are full of all kinds of deceit and trickery. Will you never stop perverting the right ways of the Lord?"[1] That is about all the politeness such people should have when they deny God's truth. We start with this assumption: we will prove that the Bible is God's word, but we are not

1 Acts 13:10 (NIV).

going to prove God's word. If you do not like to believe it, we will shake your hand, and say "Goodbye." We will not argue with you. The gospel has gained little by discussion.

The greatest piece of folly on earth has been to send a man around the country, to follow up on another who has been lecturing on infidelity just to make himself famous. Why, let them lecture on; this is a free country; why should we follow them around? The truth will win the day. Christianity need not wish for controversy; it is strong enough for it, if it wishes it; but that is not God's way.

God's direction is, "Preach, teach, dogmatize." Do not stand disputing; claim a divine mission; tell people that God says it, and leave it there. Say to them, "He that believes shall be saved, and he that does not believe shall be damned," and when you have done that, you have done enough. For what reason should our missionaries stand disputing with Brahmins? Why should they be wasting their time by attempting to refute first this dogma, and then another of heathenism? Why not just go and say, "I declare to you that you ignorantly worship your God. Believe me, and you will be saved; don't believe me, and the Bible says you are lost." And then, having thus asserted God's word, say, "I leave it, I declare it to you; it is a thing for you to believe, not a thing for you to reason about."

Religion is not a thing merely for your intellect;

to prove the greatness of your own talent upon; by making a syllogism[1] on it. It is a thing that demands your faith. As a messenger of heaven, I demand that faith; if you do not choose to give it, on your own head be your doom, if there be such; if there be not, you are prepared to risk it. But I have done my duty; I have told you the truth; that is enough, and there I leave it.

Christian, instead of disputing, let me tell you how to prove your religion! Live it out! Live it out! Give the external as well as the internal evidence; give the external evidence of your own life. You are sick; there is your neighbor who laughs at religion; let him come into your house. When he was sick, he said, "Send for the doctor," and there he was fretting, fuming and making all manner of noises. When you are sick, send for him; tell him that you are resigned to the Lord's will; that you will kiss the rod of correction; that you will take the cup and drink it, because your Father gives it.

You need not make a boast of this, or it will lose all its power, but do it because you cannot help doing it. Your neighbor will say, *"There* is something in such a religion as that." And when you come to the borders of the grave—he was there once, and you heard how he shrieked, and how frightened he was—give him your hand and say to him, "I have a Christ who will do to die by! I have a religion that

---

1 Syllogism—the regular logical form of every argument, consisting of three propositions.

will make me sing in the night." Let him hear how you can sing, "Victory, victory, victory!" through him that loved you. I tell you, we may preach fifty thousand sermons to prove the gospel, but we shall not prove it half as well as you will through singing in the night. Keep a cheerful face; keep a happy heart; keep a contented spirit; keep your eyes bright and your heart aloft, and you will prove Christianity better than all the Butlers,[1] and all the wise men who ever lived. Give them the "analogy" of a holy life and then you will prove religion to them; give them the "evidences" of internal piety, developed externally, and you will give the best possible proof of Christianity. Try and sing songs in the night, for they are so rare that if you can sing them, you will honor your God, and bless your friends.

I have been addressing all this time, the children of God, and now there is a sad turn that this subject must take; just a word or so, and then I will be done. There is a night coming in which there will be no songs of joy—a night when a song shall be sung of which misery shall be the subject, set to the music of wailing and gnashing of teeth; there is a night coming when calamity, unutterable misery, shall be the theme of an awful, terrific *miserere*,[2]

---

1 A reference to Joseph Butler (1692–1752) who wrote important works of Christian apologetics.
2 Miserere—Latin for "have mercy"; a musical composition adapted to the 51ST Psalm.

when the orchestra shall be composed of dammed people, and howling fiends, and yelling demons. Be warned, I speak of what I know, and am declaring the Scriptures. There is a night coming for the poor soul within this house tonight, and unless they repent, it will be a night in which they will have to sigh, and cry, and moan, and groan forever.

"Who is that?" you say.

It is you my friend, if you are godless and Christless.

"What!" you say, "am I in danger of hell-fire?"

In danger, my friend! Yes, more, you are condemned already, the Bible says so.

You say, "And can you leave me without telling me what I must do to be saved? Can you believe that I am in danger of perishing, and not speak to me?"

I trust not; I hope I shall never preach a sermon without speaking to the nonbeliever. How I love them! Swearer, your mouth is black with profanities now, and if you die, you must go on blaspheming throughout eternity, and be punished for it throughout eternity! But listen to me, blasphemer! Do you repent? Do you feel yourself to have sinned against God? Do you feel a desire to be saved? Listen! you may be saved; you may be saved as much as anyone who is here now. There is another; she has sinned against God enormously, and she blushes even now while I mention her case; do you repent of your sin? Then there is pardon for you; remember him who said, "Go, and sin no more." Drunkard! But a little while ago you were reeling down the street, and now you repent; drunkard, there is hope for you.

"Well," you say, "what shall I do to be saved?"

Let me tell you again the old way of salvation; it is, "Believe on the Lord Jesus Christ, and you shall be saved." We can get no further than that, do what we will; this is the sum and substance of the gospel. "He that believes in the Lord Jesus Christ, and is baptized shall be saved." So says the Savior himself. Do you ask,

"What is it to believe?"

Am I to tell you again? I cannot tell you except that it is to look to Christ. Do you see the Savior there? He is hanging on the cross; there are his dear hands, pierced with nails, fastened to a tree as if they were waiting for your tardy footsteps, because you would not come. *Do* you see his dear head there? It is hanging on his breast, as if he would lean over, and *kiss* your poor soul. Do you see his blood, gushing from his head, his hands, his feet, his side? It is running after you because he well knew that you would never run after him. Sinner, to be saved, all you have to do is to look at that Man! Can't you do it now?

"No," you say, "I do not believe that will save me."

My poor friend, try it! I urgently ask you to try it, and if you do not succeed, when you have tried it—I will be bondsman for my Lord—here, take me, bind me and I will suffer your doom for you. This I will venture to say—if you cast yourself on Christ and he deserts you, I will be willing to go halves with you in all your misery and woe. For he will never do it; never, *never*, NEVER!

> "No sinner was ever empty sent back,
>   Who came seeking mercy for Jesus' sake."[1]

I plead with you, therefore, try him, and you shall not try him in vain; you shall find him "able to save completely those who come to God through him."[2] And you shall be saved now, and saved forever. May God give you his blessing; and may you, my dear brothers and sisters, have songs in the night!

---

1 A quote from *Thy Mercy, My God, Is the Theme of My Song* by John Stocker.
2 See Hebrews 7:25 (NIV).

NOTES

NOTES

MAN'S QUESTIONS & GOD'S ANSWERS

Am I accountable to God?
Each of us will give an account of himself to God. ROMANS 14:12 (NIV).

Has God seen all my ways?
Everything is uncovered and laid bare before the eyes of him to whom we must give account. HEBREWS 4:13 (NIV).

Does he charge me with sin?
But the Scripture declares that the whole world is a prisoner of sin. GALATIANS 3:22 (NIV).
All have sinned and fall short of the glory of God. ROMANS 3:23 (NIV).

Will he punish sin?
The soul who sins is the one who will die. EZEKIEL 18:4 (NIV).
For the wages of sin is death, but the gift of God is eternal life in Christ Jesus our Lord. ROMANS 6:23 (NIV).

Must I perish?
He is patient with you, not wanting anyone to perish, but everyone to come to repentance. 2 PETER 3:9 (NIV).

How can I escape?
Believe in the Lord Jesus, and you will be saved. ACTS 16:31 (NIV).

Is he able to save me?
Therefore he is able to save completely those who come to God through him. HEBREWS 7:25 (NIV).

Is he willing?
Christ Jesus came into the world to save sinners. 1 TIMOTHY 1:15 (NIV).

Am I saved on believing?
Whoever believes in the Son has eternal life, but whoever rejects the Son will not see life, for God's wrath remains on him. JOHN 3:36 (NIV).

Can I be saved now?
Now is the time of God's favor, now is the day of salvation. 2 CORINTHIANS 6:2 (NIV).

As I am?
Whoever comes to me I will never drive away. JOHN 6:37 (NIV).

Shall I not fall away?
Him who is able to keep you from falling. JUDE 1:24 (NIV).

If saved, how should I live?
Those who live should no longer live for themselves but for him who died for them and was raised again. 2 CORINTHIANS 5:15 (NIV).

What about death and eternity?
I am going there to prepare a place for you. I will come back and take you to be with me that you also may be where I am. JOHN 14:2-3 (NIV).

www.ingramcontent.com/pod-product-compliance
Lightning Source LLC
Chambersburg PA
CBHW020442030426
42337CB00014B/1353